ASTEROID IMPACT

◆ DOUGLAS HENDERSON ◆

Dial Books for Young Readers New York

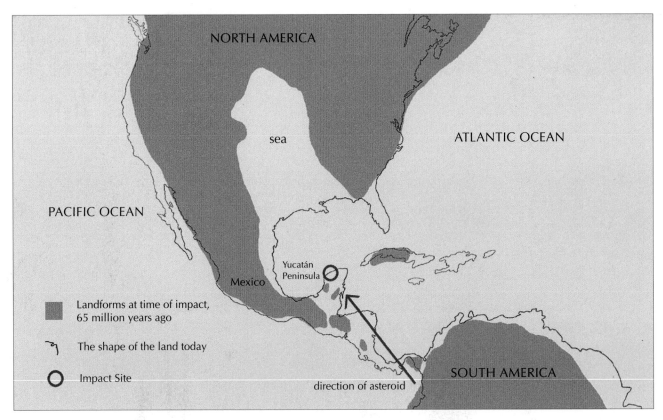

NORTH AMERICA

ATLANTIC OCEAN

sea

PACIFIC OCEAN

Yucatán
Peninsula

Mexico

Landforms at time of impact,
65 million years ago

The shape of the land today

Impact Site

direction of asteroid

SOUTH AMERICA

Map of Impact Site

Published by Dial Books for Young Readers
A division of Penguin Putnam Inc.
345 Hudson Street • New York, New York 10014

Copyright © 2000 by Douglas Henderson
All rights reserved. Designed by Nancy R. Leo-Kelly
Printed in Hong Kong on acid-free paper
10 9 8 7 6 5 4 3 2 1

Library of Congress Cataloging in Publication Data
Henderson, Douglas.

Asteroid impact/by Douglas Henderson.
p.   cm.
Summary: Text and illustrations explore the theory that the collision of an
asteroid with Earth ended the Cretaceous Period and caused the extinction of
the dinosaurs.
ISBN 0-8037-2500-0
1. Dinosaurs—Juvenile literature. 2. Extinction (Biology)—Juvenile literature.
3. Asteroids—Collisions with Earth—Juvenile literature.
[1. Dinosaurs. 2. Extinction (Biology). 3. Asteroids.] I. Title.
QE862.D5H535   2000   567.9—dc21   99-38263   CIP

Special thanks to Charles L. Pillmore of the U.S. Geological Survey (retired) for checking the facts in this book, providing technical papers,
and for many discussions about impact phenomena. Thanks also to Cindy Kane for letting me blow up the world. —D. H.

title page illustration: A *Tyrannosaurus rex* (meat-eating dinosaur) with typical Cretaceous plants.

✦ Plesiosaurs (marine reptiles) and a group of *Pteranodon* (flying reptiles)

Setting the Stage

Sixty-five million years ago, Earth was alive with great reptiles. Pterosaurs soared in the air above endless beaches and crashing waves. Marine reptiles glided through the seas on winglike paddles, their toothy heads breaking the water's surface to breathe. On the land, dinosaurs roamed the forests and river plains.

◆ A group of *Struthiomimus* (ostrich-like dinosaurs) pass two *Triceratops* (horned dinosaurs).

There were herds of duckbills and horned ceratopsians. There were armored ankylosaurs and swift, long-necked dinosaurs that looked very much like ostriches. Great meat-eaters with huge jaws and teeth hunted their prey, standing motionless in the shade of groves and striding the banks of streams. Rivers large and small flowed to the sea, enclosed by grand trees of sequoia, cypress, sassafras, and tulip poplar. The air was filled with the sounds of birds, frogs, and insects, and even the scurrying of small mammals.

This was late in the Cretaceous Period, a time in Earth's history when the world was home to remarkable living things. But the late Cretaceous was about to come to an abrupt end.

4

◆ Two *Nanotyrannus* (meat-eating dinosaurs) stalk a group of *Anatotitan* (duck-billed dinosaurs).

Invisible in the sky, an asteroid was drawing close to Earth. It was 6 miles across and traveling 18 miles a second. It had passed far beneath the moon's south pole, drifting past its landscape of huge impact craters in just minutes. Then it left the moon behind as it fell toward Earth.

✦ The asteroid passes over large impact craters near the moon's south pole.

The asteroid had once been a part of the asteroid belt, a region between the orbits of Mars and Jupiter where thousands of asteroids circle the sun. Made of stone, or nickel and iron, or a mix of both stone and metal, asteroids are rubble from a planet that never formed. Some asteroids are less than a mile across. Some are much larger. A few are as big as very small planets.

Because of their small size, the asteroids' orbits are easily disturbed. Jupiter is an enormous planet, and its gravity can pull smaller asteroids in new directions. The gravity of larger asteroids can also tug on smaller ones that pass close by. And from time to time, asteroids can collide and be nudged into new orbits.

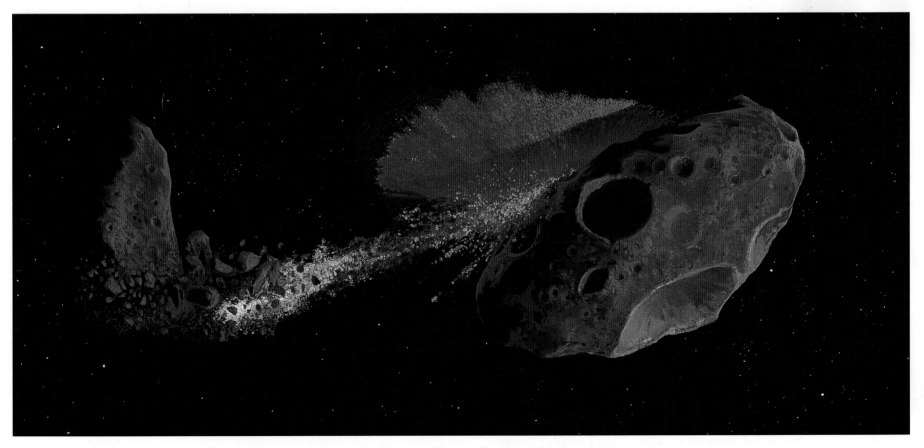

✦ Leaving a spray of ejected dust, one asteroid grazes another in the asteroid belt.

By such events, some asteroids can be pulled or pushed out of the asteroid belt to fall closer to the sun. They can wander in long, elliptical orbits that cross the paths of Mars and the other inner planets, including Earth. These asteroids can hit the planets—and on rare occasions they do.

Sixty-five million years ago, one of these wandering asteroids was crossing Earth's orbit. It may have circled the sun this way for thousands of years, perhaps coming close to Earth many times. But on one particular orbit around the sun, the asteroid and Earth approached the same point at the same time.

The Target

Our solar system existed then very much as it does today. And among the nine planets, Earth was unique. Only Earth had vast oceans of liquid water and circled the sun at a distance of 93,000,000 miles. The other planets, circling closer to the sun or farther away, traveled in extremes of great heat or cold. Sunlight that reached Earth had just enough energy to keep the oceans warm and to carry clouds and storms across the continents on tropical breezes.

✦ A mosasaur (marine reptile), three *Xiphactinus* (large predatory fish), and a juvenile plesiosaur.

Billions of years ago, life started on the early Earth and began a great work of engineering. Powered by sunlight, simple plants stripped oxygen from water molecules and released it into the air, where no free oxygen had existed before. The early atmosphere was rich in carbon dioxide. This gas was used along with calcium by countless tiny sea creatures to make their shells. Those shells rained upon the sea floor and formed into layers of rock many miles thick, trapping the carbon dioxide. In time, the chemistry of Earth's air, water, and land changed and became a place where life could grow and flourish. Down through time, life changed into a wilderness of different forms.

But the flourishing life of Earth could be disrupted by natural events. Slowly or quickly, many kinds of plants and animals could become extinct, changing life on Earth forever. The greatest extinction ever known occurred long before dinosaurs existed. This was 250 million years ago, at the end of the Permian Period. Great, long-lasting volcanic eruptions changed Earth's climate, and most of Earth's life died out. After this great extinction, the Mesozoic Era—the time when dinosaurs lived—began.

Now the Mesozoic was to end with another great extinction. An asteroid impact would bring a catastrophe to the late Cretaceous world. The dinosaurs would vanish. So would the marine reptiles, the pterosaurs, and many other creatures.

Well before dawn in the dark southern sky of North America, a new object appeared. It shone in the night like a second moon, only bigger and oddly shaped. It slowly grew in size. It was an asteroid 300 miles away, and it was about to strike Earth.

✦ The approaching asteroid shines in the night sky of Mexico above a tyrannosaur.

The Asteroid's Energy

The impact of the asteroid on Earth would release an enormous amount of energy, and most of the terrible events that followed would be driven by this energy. What *is* energy? A simple answer is that energy is the ability to do work. An asteroid speeding along in open space does not appear to be doing any work at all. But if an object 6 miles in diameter hit Earth, it could do a lot of work. In only a few seconds, enough energy would be released to dig a crater 50 miles across. Enough heat and pressure would be produced to throw billions of tons of molten rock and dust high above Earth's atmosphere.

Where would all the energy in the asteroid come from? In part, it would come from its motion. This kind of energy is called kinetic energy. The faster an object moves, the more kinetic energy it has.

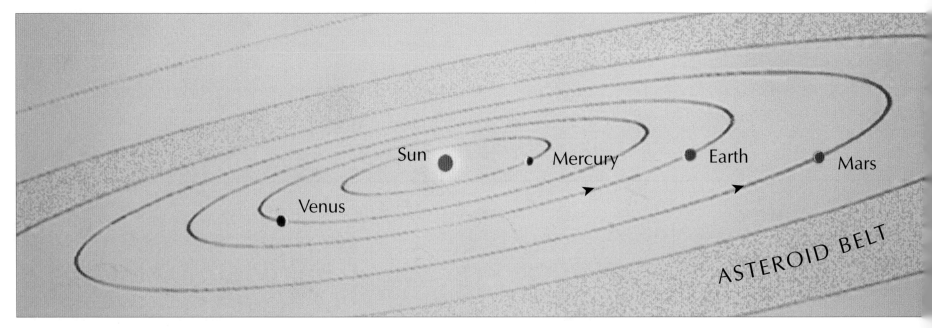

◆ Position of the asteroid belt

An asteroid in the asteroid belt orbits the sun at about 10 miles a second, or 36,000 miles an hour. It has traveled this way for 4.5 billion years, ever since it formed from the dust that created the solar system. Drawn by gravity, most of this dust came together to form the sun. The remaining dust circled the sun and slowly built the comets, the planets and their moons, and the asteroids. Just as the orbiting planets were held in the sun's gravity, the asteroids also inherited the ancient motion of this orbiting dust as they formed.

In addition, an asteroid that crossed the path of Earth would move toward the sun for part of its orbit. The sun's gravity would cause it to travel faster and faster. Earth's gravity would also pull on the asteroid, adding to its speed. The force of gravity is the source of an asteroid's enormous stored-up energy.

The kinetic energy in an asteroid 6 miles across and traveling 18 miles a second is so great, it is nearly impossible to imagine. An example can help show why.

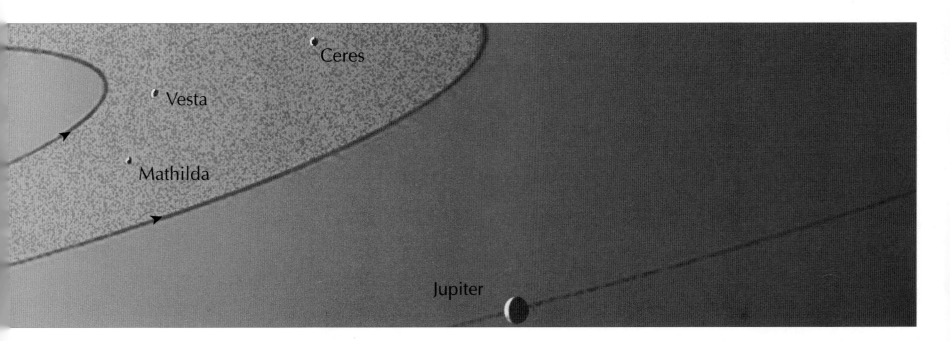

Imagine that we can repeatedly send a car that weighs about a ton (2,000 pounds) into a block of solid concrete the size of a house. Each impact will be 10 times faster than the one before it.

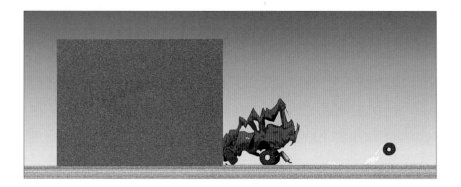

The first impact is at a speed of 60 miles per hour (mph). The energy released has enough force to change the shape of the car. The concrete wall might show a scratch.

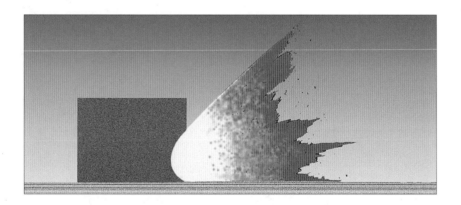

The second impact is at 600 mph, the speed of a jet airplane. Although the speed has increased 10 times, the kinetic energy has increased 100 times (10 x 10). The impact is far more violent. The car doesn't just change shape; it tears itself apart into small metal fragments. The impact would leave a crater in the concrete block.

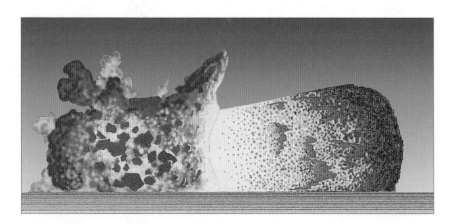

The third impact is at 6,000 mph, the speed of a rocket. Again, the speed has increased 10 times and the energy has increased 100 times. Now the impact releases so much energy that the car flies apart into tiny molten pieces. The heat and pressure are enough to fracture the concrete block into a mound of rubble.

The last impact is at 60,000 mph. This is the speed of an asteroid traveling toward Earth. Although the car still weighs one ton, the energy released from this impact is a million times (1000 x 1000) greater than the energy released by the car's impact at 60 mph. The energy of the impact would travel as a shock wave forward through the concrete and backward through the car. As it passed, it would pulverize and quickly heat everything to thousands of degrees Fahrenheit. Both the car and the concrete block would vaporize into a hot cloud of expanding gas. A few miles away, radiant heat from the bright flash of the explosion would feel like warm sunlight on your face. A bubble of hot vapor looking like a fireball would rise up into the sky. As it cooled, the hot vapor would condense into a dust like sand or fine powder. It would rain to the ground and drift on the wind. When the dust settled, the car and the concrete block would be gone. In their place would be a shallow crater perhaps hundreds of feet across.

If an object weighing just 1 ton and traveling at high speed could cause such a large explosion, what would happen if an asteroid 6 miles across and weighing a trillion tons struck Earth at high speed?

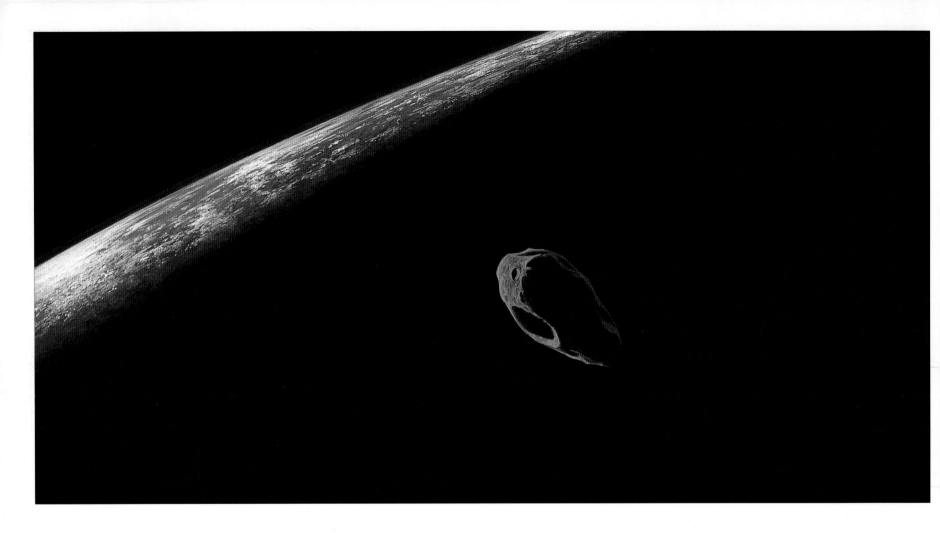

Impact

Shining in sunlight, the asteroid approached the night side of Earth. Entering Earth's shadow in the last seconds before impact, the asteroid grew dim and suddenly vanished into the darkness. Then, over what is now southern Mexico, it plowed into Earth's atmosphere, and the night became like day.

✦ The asteroid plunges through Earth's atmosphere as a tylosaur (marine reptile) leaps above the sea.

An ocean of air slammed up against the asteroid and heated to a fiery brilliance. Now the asteroid was a huge white ball 4 times brighter than the sun, sweeping across the sky. A great heat fell upon the water and land and forests below.

The asteroid traveled through Earth's atmosphere in 4 seconds. Then it plunged into a tropical sea coast. In a fraction of a second, it passed below Earth's surface. A great crater formed, expanding out and downward at several miles per second.

◆ The asteroid passes below Earth's surface in a fraction of a second.

A fantastic explosion began to unfold. In a blinding light, a vapor plume of superheated gas and dust rushed up and outward from the widening crater. Within the plume, hundreds of billions of tons of vaporized rock and seawater rose up and away from Earth. The growing explosion pushed the atmosphere aside.

✦ Viewed above a sea of clouds, the vapor plume rises from the growing crater.

✦ The leading edge of the vapor plume spreads rapidly over land and sea.

The shock wave of the expanding vapor plume raced out over the land and sea at 18 miles per second, compressing the air before it into burning light. As it advanced, its glowing wall ripped away the earth and water down to bedrock, destroying everything in its path.

The asteroid vaporized a second after impact, coating the inside of the crater, then rose with the expanding plume. Hidden deep within the hot cloud, the crater was growing 20, then 30, then 40 miles across.

✦ The expanding vapor plume pushes up through the atmosphere.

Ten seconds after the impact, the vapor plume rocketed up above the atmosphere and, in the cold vacuum of space, began to grow hundreds of miles across.

Hot gas continued to erupt from the crater. Limestone rocks deep within it had vaporized into hot carbon dioxide gas. This gas joined the growing explosion, throwing more dust and molten rock above the atmosphere.

As the crater stopped expanding, island-sized blocks of land and walls of debris rose and fell back down. Huge, hot clouds of mud, gas, and boulders poured out over the land for hundreds of miles beyond the crater's rim. Where this debris spilled into the sea, huge waves began to build. Growing thousands of feet high, these waves rolled north across the open sea toward the coasts of what are now Texas and Arkansas.

◆ Hot clouds of mud, gas, and rock pour out from the crater and plunge into the sea.

Now the crater, 25 miles deep, was collapsing. Molten earth rushed up from below, and the crater walls fell in. Slabs of land slid into the enormous hole, and the crater continued to grow until it was more than 110 miles across. Within the crater, glowing waves towered above a sea of molten rock thousands of feet deep.

A minute after impact, the atmosphere had slowed the spreading vapor plume. But it continued to climb and expand high above Earth. The top of the great cloud rose above Earth's shadow and into the sunlight, gleaming in space. By this time, the plume's outer shell had cooled into smooth white clouds of ice crystals. Within the plume, vaporized rock and water began to condense into blankets of speeding dust and ice that spread out above Earth in every direction. Earth's gravity pulled on this debris. Some of the dust continued to travel upward for many hours. But most of the debris, called ejecta, was beginning to curve back toward Earth.

✦ Now nearly 500 miles high, the vapor plume continues to expand.

Shock waves from the asteroid's impact had raced outward through the water, land, and air. They rippled across the surface of Earth for thousands of miles, causing earthquakes and carrying the thunderous sound of the impact.

Illuminating the early-morning sky of North America, the vapor plume was rising high above the southern horizon. Then, with a roar, the first shock waves reached the Texas coast, and the

◆ As the bright vapor plume widens across the southern horizon, a group of *Torosaurus* (horned dinosaurs) are caught in an earthquake.

lowlands began to shake. The earthquake toppled trees, and limbs crashed to the ground. The water in lakes and rivers heaved and sloshed over their banks. The vapor plume was expanding all across the southern sky. Against the glow, odd, dark clouds and shadows of approaching ejecta climbed up the sky from the south. As the ground continued to shake, the horizon began to glow—first red, then blinding white.

✦ Vast clouds of dust heat up and glow as they plunge back into Earth's atmosphere.

Now billions of tons of ejecta—dust and melted rock—fell back to Earth. Traveling at several miles per second, these dark blankets of dust began to plunge down through the atmosphere. Friction caused the air and dust to heat up and blaze white-hot. The heat radiated to the ground 50 miles below. Over the oceans, the surface of the water began to steam. Over land, forests smoldered and burned. The sky became an oven, and only places under thick cloud cover escaped the broiling heat.

Spreading outward, the first fiery ejecta returned to Earth only minutes after the impact. It fell over Mexico, then Texas. Minutes later it reached Wyoming, then Montana, then Alberta and Saskatchewan, Canada. All across North America, huge fires started and clouds of smoke and soot rose into the air. The ejecta fell for hours. Dust and tiny spheres of melted rock fell from the sky to the ground all over Earth's surface.

✦ Fires across North America send clouds of smoke and soot high into the sky.

The tall waves produced by the impact rolled swiftly northward across the Gulf of Mexico. As they reached the shallow coasts of North America, the waves swelled up still higher. They swept over the coasts and rolled on over the land, crashing upon the landscape of burning forests. Vast coastal plains and tropical forests vanished beneath the waves. When the water flowed back to the sea, it dragged soil, boulders, and the remains of the forests with it. Under clouds of dust and smoke, the land grew dark, hiding the scenes of destruction that stretched for thousands of miles from the asteroid's impact crater.

High above the devastation, the vapor plume had grown larger than Earth, becoming a cold, thin cloud. As gravity pulled it back down, the huge cloud swallowed Earth in a haze of descending ice and dust.

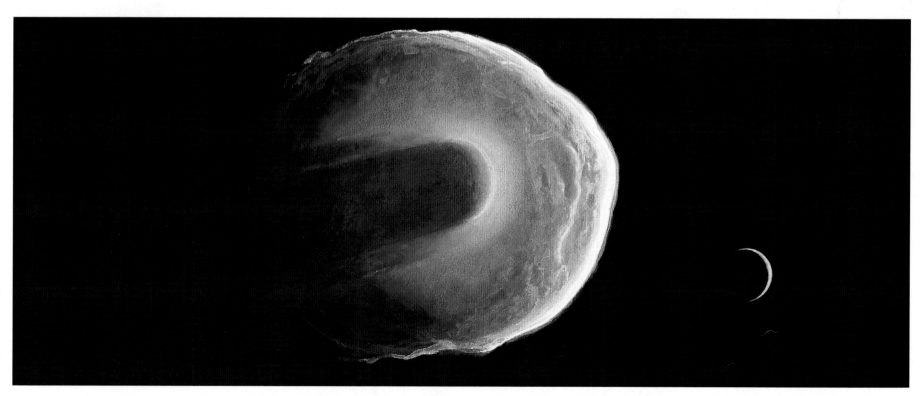

◆ Earth is surrounded by a huge cloud of falling dust and ice.

Aftermath

The asteroid's impact threw billions of tons of dust above Earth's atmosphere. Most of it soon fell back down. But the smallest, lightest particles did not quickly fall to the ground. Instead, they floated high in the atmosphere and mixed with the smoke and soot from the fires below. This dust circled the globe, carried on the winds. As the dust spread, the sky grew gloomy, then as dark as night. For many months, the dust blocked the sunlight and reflected it back into space. A long, unbroken darkness fell over Earth's surface.

Life on Earth has always needed the energy of sunlight to live. From the great sequoia forests on land to the tiny, single-celled algae that filled the seas, the plants of the Cretaceous used sunlight to make their own food. In turn, the plants fed the many kinds of animals on Earth. Even the big, meat-eating predators needed to eat plant-eating animals to live.

Now the sunlight was gone. In the darkness, plants did not have the energy they needed to grow. They could no longer release oxygen into the air or remove the carbon dioxide. And they could not produce any food. In the oceans, vast numbers of tiny, single-celled plants and the tiny, single-celled animals that ate them were the source of food for all the larger sea creatures. Many single-celled creatures died in the darkness. In a short time, on land and in the sea, much of life began to starve.

✦ Dust, smoke, and a growing darkness surround titanosaurs (long-necked plant-eating dinosaurs) in India.

With sunlight blocked by the dust, Earth began to cool. Temperatures everywhere fell below freezing. Together with the settling soot and ash from dying fires, snow fell, blanketing the land. To a once warm, tropical world came a long, dark winter.

✦ A dead tyrannosaur in Alberta, Canada, lies in a dark, cold world of falling snow and ash.

The effects of the asteroid's impact were far from over. The chemistry of the atmosphere had been changed.

Earth's air had been cooked by the great heat produced by the asteroid's impact and the hot ejecta debris raining back through the atmosphere. The heat baked new compounds from the air's oxygen and nitrogen. Nitric acid formed as a result. This mixed with water vapor in the atmosphere and fell to the ground and seas as acid rain. The high acidity dissolved the shells of sea creatures large and small. On land, many plants and animals died.

The heat produced other compounds as well. Sulfur from rocks vaporized by the impact formed clouds of sulfuric acid high in the atmosphere. These clouds circled Earth like the bright, reflective clouds of sulfuric acid that surround the planet Venus.

In time, the dust settled and the sky began to clear. Sunlight again reached Earth's surface and daylight returned. But acid-rich clouds continued to reflect sunlight back into space, keeping Earth cold for decades.

Finally, over time, the world grew warm—much too warm. When the asteroid struck Earth and plunged below the surface, it destroyed deep, thick layers of limestone rock. The impact released huge amounts of the rock's carbon dioxide into the atmosphere. The carbon dioxide trapped even more energy from the sunlight. Earth became terribly hot for hundreds of years.

From the first seconds of the asteroid's arrival until many centuries afterward, Earth became a place where life found it difficult to survive. Many kinds of plants and animals that had flourished during the Cretaceous vanished.

✦ A small mammal looks out over a scene of recovering ferns in a ruined forest.

For reasons no one knows, many kinds of living things were able to survive. In time, the effects of the asteroid impact diminished and the world healed. The forests returned. The seas again filled with tiny algae, all busily turning sunlight and carbon dioxide into food. Earth once more became a haven for life. But the Cretaceous had come to an end. The dinosaurs were gone.

Some 10 million years would pass before large plant-eaters would again move among the forests and plains of Earth. When they did appear, they were not dinosaurs. Instead, they were big mammals, preyed upon by mammal predators. The asteroid impact had cleared away much of Earth's long history of life and opened the next chapter of time for new life. Mammals now flourished. Over the next 50 million years, they diversified into many new forms, including horses, cats, elephants, and whales. And one story in this new Age of Mammals is the appearance of human beings.

✦ A *Uintatherium* (a mammal) in a semi-tropical Wyoming forest.

A Look to the Future

Could another asteroid hit Earth and wreck the world we live in? Yes. Asteroids still pass by Earth from time to time. A small asteroid exploded in the air over Siberia in 1908 and leveled a forest over a distance of many miles. It had the force of a large atomic bomb, and it was only by chance that it did not explode over a city.

However, the chances of a large asteroid or comet striking Earth are very small. Earth is 8,000 miles in diameter. As big as that may seem, compared to the vast space Earth travels through, our planet is a very small target.

✦ A small asteroid explodes over Siberia, leveling a forest.

Earth has been hit by asteroids and comets many times during its billions of years of natural history. The faint remains of craters are found scattered across Earth's surface. Some of these impacts occurred after the dinosaurs became extinct—but none were even half the size of the asteroid that struck Earth 65 million years ago.

Some people believe we should be thinking about the possibility of asteroids colliding with Earth. They hope we will be watchful enough to see an asteroid or comet coming long before it arrives. Maybe then we will have time to decide how to reach out and stop it.

Human beings bring something new to the story of life on Earth. We can imagine a future and then prepare for it. Perhaps someday we will learn how to change the course of an asteroid, just as natural forces have been doing for billions of years.

◆ ◆ ◆ ◆

Asteroid Questions and Answers

Q: Was it a comet or an asteroid that struck Earth 65 million years ago?

A: Scientists don't know. The energy released by the impact of either a comet or an asteroid would produce the same destructive effects. If a comet hit Earth, it would have come from the most distant region of the solar system. Far beyond the outer planets, countless millions of comets orbit the sun. They are made of rock, dust, frozen water, and frozen gases. As large as mountains, some of these comets travel closer to the sun and wander among the planets.

Unlike comets, asteroids have no frozen water or gases. They are more solid, having formed much like the planets during a time of great heat and repeated collisions early in the history of the solar system. I have chosen to portray an asteroid colliding with Earth 65 million years ago, rather than a comet, because there are more asteroids than comets near Earth. But this choice is only a guess. Perhaps someday scientists will have a surer answer.

Q: How do we know about the impact that ended the Cretaceous Period?

A: The evidence first came from a thin layer of rock that marks the boundary between Cretaceous ("K" for short) rocks and Tertiary ("T") rocks. This layer is called the "K/T boundary." It formed when the last Cretaceous sediments were laid down by ancient streams, rivers, and oceans.

Scientists had known for a long time that fossils of dinosaurs and many other kinds of Cretaceous animals and plants were found below the K/T boundary, but that no evidence of their fossils could be found above the boundary. This thin layer of rock represents the end of the Mesozoic Era, when the dinosaurs became extinct. But why they vanished had always puzzled scientists.

In 1977, Dr. Walter Alvarez and other scientists began to examine a thin clay layer at the K/T boundary in the mountains of central Italy. They found an unusually high concentration of a rare metal called iridium. They then looked for iridium at other K/T boundary sites around the world—and they found it there also.

Iridium is rare in Earth's crust. But it is common in meteorites—the term for objects that fall to Earth from space. Since meteorites are the remains of asteroids and comets, the concentration of iridium at the K/T boundary suggested to the Alvarez team that some huge object had fallen to Earth from the sky 65 million years ago. From the amount of iridium deposited in the boundary, they eventually estimated the size of the asteroid or comet to be about 6 miles in diameter.

The Alvarez team suggested an asteroid impact to explain the disappearance of the dinosaurs and other forms of life that became extinct at the end of the Cretaceous Period. Since their discovery, iridium has been found at the K/T boundary at more than 100 sites around the world.

Q: Was any other evidence for the great impact found?
A: Yes. When Dr. Alvarez first found the iridium in the K/T boundary, many scientists did not accept his theories. But as Alvarez and other scientists began to look for more evidence, they found it.

Strange, small grains of the mineral quartz were found at all of the K/T boundary sites. Under a microscope, rows of fracture marks can be seen within each grain of this dust. These marks indicate shock—sudden and intense pressure. Shocked quartz was already known from ancient impact craters on Earth. Only the intense pressure caused by the impact of very fast-moving objects could produce the kind of shocked quartz found in the K/T boundary.

Across North America, scientists found small spheres of melted rock in the sediments at K/T boundary sites. The melted rock was evidence of dust and gravel that had been thrown a great distance and exposed to intense heat. And they found other evidence of a huge impact in North America. Sediments found on the ocean floor suggested that great waves had traveled across shallow Cretaceous seas. Soot in the K/T boundary layer indicated that fires had burned all across North America. And just above the last Cretaceous sediments deposited on land, scientists found big increases in fossil fern spores. They were evidence of an abundant growth of fern plants following a period of terrible devastation.

Then scientists learned about an impact crater buried in sediments in the Yucatán Peninsula of eastern Mexico. The crater is the correct age and about the right size to have been caused by the impact that ended the Cretaceous. It is 65 million years old and more than 110 miles across—one of the largest craters ever discovered on Earth.

The search for evidence led to another remarkable thing. Geologists and paleontologists began to talk to astronomers and physicists, scientists with whom they did not often exchange ideas. Knowledge of the solar system, including its wandering asteroids and comets, has now become a part of the science of geology. It has become important to learn how impact craters form and how the sudden release of such enormous energy can cause great changes on Earth. The evidence of these fantastic events is being found in the rocks, mixed with the story of Earth's ancient life.

Index/Bibliography

Boldface page numbers refer to illustrations.

ALVAREZ, WALTER. *T. rex and the Crater of Doom.* Princeton: Princeton University Press, 1997.

DINGUS, LOWELL and TIMOTHY ROWE. *The Mistaken Extinction: Dinosaur Evolution and the Origin of Birds.* New York: W. H. Freeman and Company, 1997.

RUSSELL, DALE A. *An Odyssey in Time: The Dinosaurs of North America.* Minocqua, WI: Northword Press, Inc., 1989.

SAGAN, CARL and ANN DRUYAN. *Comet.* New York: Ballantine Books, 1985, 1997.

VERSCHUUR, GERRIT L. *Impact! The Threat of Comets & Asteroids.* New York: Oxford University Press, 1996.